DOMINOES
BASIC RULES & VARIATIONS

Reiner F. Müller

Sterling Publishing Co., Inc. New York

Library of Congress Cataloging-in-Publication Data

Müller, Reiner F.
  [Spielend Domino lernen. English]
  Dominoes : basic rules & variations / Reiner F. Müller.
      p.   cm.
  Translated from German.
  Includes index.
  ISBN 0-8069-3880-3
  1. Dominoes—Rules. I. Title.
GV1467.M85   1995
795.3—dc20   95-30974
                                                  CIP
                                                  AC

Published 1995 by Sterling Publishing Company, Inc.
387 Park Avenue South, New York, N.Y. 10016
Originally published and © 1987 in Germany by
Econ Taschenbuch Verlag GmbH, Düsseldorf
This edition published by Falken-Verlag GmbH
under the title *Spielend Domino lernen*
© 1994 by Falken-Verlag GmbH Niedernhausen/Ts.
English translation © 1995 by Sterling Publishing Co., Inc.
Distributed in Canada by Sterling Publishing
c/o Canadian Manda Group, One Atlantic Avenue, Suite 105
Toronto, Ontario, Canada M6K 3E7
Distributed in Great Britain and Europe by Cassell PLC
Wellington House, 125 Strand, London WC2R 0BB, England
Distributed in Australia by Capricorn Link (Australia) Pty Ltd.
P.O. Box 6651, Baulkham Hills, Business Centre, NSW 2153, Australia
Manufactured in the United States of America

Sterling ISBN 0-8069-3880-3

Contents

Preface

Everyone recognizes the rectangular black tiles with the white dots; after all, they accompanied most of us through childhood. We remember hours of happy entertainment. Today many sets of domino tiles sit on shelves, relics of childhood. But are dominoes simply a game for children? Not at all! Dominoes is more than a children's game. Dominoes is one of the few universal games which have entertained young and old players equally for centuries. The material used to make domino sets today does not convey the same pleasure. In addition, the rules enclosed with new sets are barely intelligible. Often the manufacturer has written them carelessly. Get to know dominoes all over again: diversified, fascinating, and multifaceted.

- Solo games: Exercise for your grey cells.
- Entertainment for the whole family. Fun and suspense for all.
- Games for two: Amusement or competition.

Dominoes: The intelligent game!

We can trace the history back to the early eighteenth century. At that time, domino pieces made of ivory appeared in Italy for the first time. From there, the game spread all over Europe.

In the middle of the eighteenth century, dominoes was the most popular of all games. As the game developed, new forms mixed with old.

The starting point of all rules was probably based on the most simple style of play, Block Dominoes. Numerous variations developed, but they belong to a few major groups.

- When playing Block Dominoes, you don't "buy," i.e., you only play with the pieces you start with.
- The next group permits you to draw dominoes after the game has started.
- A third group isn't as uniform. Even the names of the games are a problem. Thus, for example, All Five is also known as Muggins, Matador is also Master Dominoes, and Maltese Cross is also called Doubles. Sebastopol is sometimes called Cyprus, but the game Fortress is also usually called Sebastopol.

We've only been able to make guesses and assumptions about the real origins of dominoes. Arabia may have been the country of

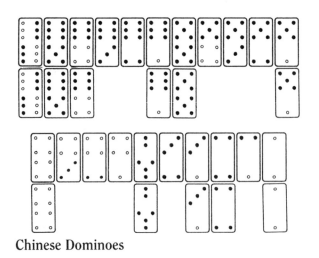

Chinese Dominoes

origin. In Egypt, it's still one of the most popular café games, but China is also a definite possibility. From China, Marco Polo could have brought it to Europe.

Many good games come from China; for example, mah-jongg, a game for four people, uses 144 pieces. By 1400, it had spread all over China. Some people consider mah-jongg to be the "great-grandfather" of dominoes. R. C. Bell, an English game researcher, believes that dominoes clearly was a Chinese invention. A set of Chinese dominoes consists of 32 pieces. There are eleven pairs of doubles, but no blanks or zeros (see picture).

Whatever its derivation, dominoes is a fantastic game. Our thanks for many entertaining hours should go to the unknown person, who invented the game.

Basic Terms

The Pieces

Domino tiles, also called bones, stones, and men, are twice as long as they are wide. A groove on the upper side divides them into two equal squares. Most squares have spots, called pips, that are similar to the spots on dice.

The squares that don't have pips are called blanks, zeroes, whites, or pales. Pieces with the same number of pips on both squares are called doubles or doublets.

The number of pips ranges from zero to six in a standard set. In the case of a large set, the pips range from zero to twelve.

Each combination of pips occurs only once in a set. The individual tiles have names. For example, the tile with a blank on one side and a one on the other would be 0-1; two and three would be 2-3; and six and six would be 6-6, a double six, or a six doublet.

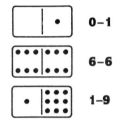

Domino Sets

The sets consist of 28 tiles, 55 tiles, or 91 tiles. The material is usually black wood or black plastic with white pips.

Buy sets in which the tiles are thick enough to stand up by themselves. You won't enjoy the game as much if the tiles are constantly falling over.

When you consider purchasing a new game, buy a set of 55 or 91 because they increase the possibilities considerably. Even though they are more difficult to handle than the smaller sets, they allow more people to participate in the game. And of course the larger sets contain all the in-between stages:

- 36 tiles (highest number is 7)
- 45 tiles (highest number is 8)

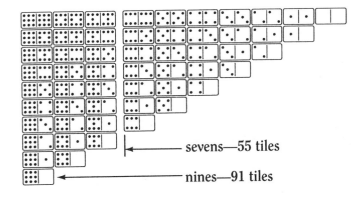

sevens—55 tiles

nines—91 tiles

The Pips

In order to be able to evaluate the situation in a game, it's important to know how often each number of spots or pips occurs. In the case of a 28-tile set, each number appears eight times: once each on six tiles and twice on the double tile.

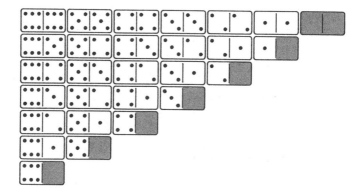

In the case of a 55-tile set, each number occurs eleven times: once each on nine tiles and twice on the double tile.

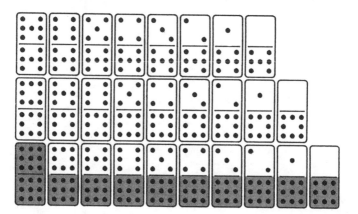

For most domino variations, the basic rules are the same.

Shuffling the Pieces

Before every game, the players shuffle, or mix, the tiles with the pips facing the table. The players' hands may not stay on the same tiles while shuffling.

Sometimes, the winner of the last game shuffles for the next one. The "boneyard," or the "reserve," is the name given to mixed tiles which are lying face down on the table.

The players draw tiles for the game from the boneyard.

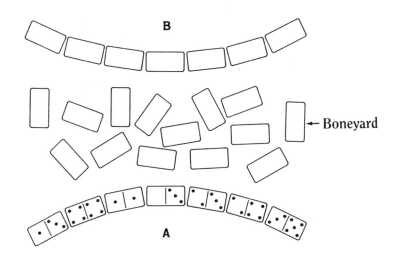

Beginning the Game

The game may begin in one of two ways: through drawing lots or through ownership of the "heavi-est" domino. A domino is heavier than another domino if it has more spots, or pips. A domino is lighter if it has fewer spots.

Drawing Lots

Each player takes one tile out of the boneyard. Whoever has the heaviest domino may begin.

The tiles are put back and mixed again.

Now the participants draw tiles for the game.

Drawing Pieces

Each player takes as many tiles as the rules permit. The person who did the mixing is the last one to pick pieces.

Each player places his pieces in front of him in such a way that the other players can't see the pits on his pieces.

The remaining tiles stay face down in the boneyard. Depending on the rules, players may "buy" tiles from the boneyard.

Opening the Game

After each player draws his tiles, the player with the heaviest double (6-6, 5-5, 4-4 . . .) begins the game by placing that piece face up in the middle of the table.

If no player has a double tile, then the player with the heaviest single tile begins.

Many people accept the rule that a player who has played a double may immediately add a second tile onto this. Before you begin, decide whether you want to follow this rule or not. If you do, then it's valid for the opening and for the entire game.

The winner of the last game always opens the succeeding game of a match.

If a round ends in a tie because it was blocked, the player who placed the last tile opens.

For all matches in this book, games open with any tile when the first player is drawn in a lot or with the heaviest double in the game.

Adding Pieces

In most domino games, players must add tiles to the free end of played tiles, matching the new squares with previously played ones having the same number of pips.

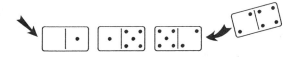

Only doubles can be placed crosswise. After each double, however, the next piece must be added lengthwise.

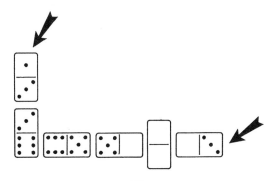

It doesn't matter what kind of figure the tiles create. But the ends have to be free so that players can add more tiles to them. The drawing shows the most common type of layout. The first player

13

opened with the 6-5. Note that the double tile was added with the dividing line next to the tile. The game may continue on both open ends.

The drawing shows an unusual type of layout. Players often prefer

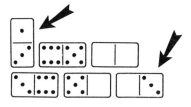

this layout for games with sets of 55 or 91 dominoes because, despite the larger number of bones, the game only requires a limited surface. This form takes a little getting used to.

The first player opened this game with the 6-5 bone, too. The arrows point to the free ends.

Passing & Buying

Once the first player has put down the first tile, the other players follow, clockwise. Every player adds a tile to one of the free ends.

Anyone who doesn't have a bone with the right number of pips must **pass** or **buy**.

Passing, also known as knocking and renouncing, means that the player cannot add on a tile. After he says, "I pass," it's the next player's turn.

When all players have to pass in a game, the game ends immediately. A game which ends this way is a **blocked** game.

If the rules permit buying, a player has to take as many tiles from the boneyard as the rules dictate or until he finds a matching tile.

When the player draws a matching tile, he adds it on.

The player has to keep all the tiles he bought, adding them to his other tiles.

In all domino games, the rules indicate whether a player may buy pieces and how many pieces a player may buy per game.

Bones in the Boneyard

Today, most players accept the rule that all tiles may be bought from the boneyard. The disadvantage is that the game lacks mystery because all tiles come into the game at some point.

In the past, the rules stated that the last two tiles in the boneyard couldn't be bought. The winner of the game received credit for the number of pips on these bones left at the end of the game.

The old rule is preferable, especially for experienced players.

End of the Game

A domino game ends when one player doesn't have any tiles left. When a player adds his last tile, he announces, "Domino."

Blocked Games

A game is blocked when none of the players is able to add another tile at either end.

Scoring

The losing players count the number of pips on their pieces. Count doublets only once; thus, 4-4 counts as only 4 points.

In the case of a blocked game, the winner is the person whose remaining tiles add up to the fewest points. If the score ends in a tie, the game doesn't count.

Since players often play several games in a row, they can use a system to determine the overall winner. The loser's total number of pips becomes points for the winner. This system works well when several people are playing.

When using this system, players have to determine the number of games to be played or the number of points to be reached (100 or 150 points). When a player reaches this, he wins the game.

When using this system, players have to determine the number of games to be played or the number of points to be reached (100 or 150 points). When a player reaches this, he wins the game.

First Example:

For simple scoring in the case of three players (A, B, C):
Game ends in victory for A.
- A: won
- B: left with 7 pips
- C: left with 12 pips
A wins the game with 19 points (7 + 12).
Game is blocked.
- A: left with 9 pips
- B: left with 3 pips
- C: left with 5 pips
B wins the game with 11 points (9 + 5 − 3).

Second Example:

For a difference-calculation in the case of three players (A, B, C):
- A: left with 9 pips
- B: left with 2 pips
- C: won
In order to create a table, draw a column for the players, a column for the points, a column for the differences, and a fourth column for the total points.
Determine the difference in points between the players: between C and B and between C and A.
Between C and B
- C: 0
- B: 2
Difference: 2
- C: +2
Between C and A
- C: 0
- A: 9
Difference: 9
- C: +9
For player C, the results are as follows:

PLAYER	A	B	C
POINTS	9	2	0
DIFFERENCE			+2
			+9
TOTAL POINTS			+11

Now we have to calculate the differences between B and A, B and C, A and B, and A and C.

Between B and A
- B: 2
- A: 9
Difference: 7
- B: +7

Between B and C
- B: 2
- C: 0
Difference: −2
- B: −2

Between A and B
- A: 9
- B: 2
Difference: −7
- A: −7

Between A and C
- A: 9
- C: 0
Difference: −9
- A: −9

This is the complete table for the example game:

PLAYER:	A	B	C
POINTS:	9	2	0
DIFFERENCE:	−7	+7	+2
	−9	−2	+9
TOTAL POINTS:	−16	+5	+11

Now you'll learn the basic rules for Block Dominoes, the classic game. Variations for other interesting games developed from this game.

Block Dominoes

You need: 28-tile set and two or more players.

- Players A and B each take eight pieces from the boneyard.
- The remaining tiles aren't used in the game.
- The player with the heaviest double tile begins. If there are no doublets, the person with the heaviest piece begins.
- The players agree on how many games they will play, or what number of points they want to play to.

The Game

- B positions his bone.
- Then it's A's turn to match a tile with the same number of pips to one of the ends of B's bone.
- The two players alternate adding on. The players may add doublets lengthwise and crosswise.
- When a player doesn't have a tile to match one of the ends, he has to pass.
- The game ends as soon as a player has added all of his tiles or when neither player can add any more pieces.
- The winner gets the difference in the number of pips.

Here is an example:

Both players have to pass. A still has a tile with 7 pips, and B still has two tiles with a total of 13 pips. A wins this game with +6 points (13–7).

Here's another example:

Players A and B drew the following pieces:

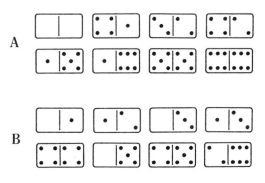

A has the heaviest double, 6-6, and starts with that piece.

A: 6-6

B: 6-2

A: 6-1

(Good move, since he has other ones.)

B: 1-3

A: 3-2

(A's move is risky, since now both ends have twos, but A has another one.)

B: 2-1

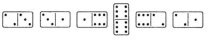

A: 1-5

(He is trying to create a way to use his 5-5.)

B: 5-4

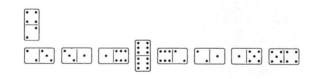

(On both ends are two fours. Of the seven men left, A has another four. The possibility that B also has another four is strong; any attempt to block is, therefore, premature.)

A: 2-4

B: 4-4

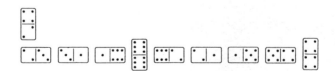

20

(For A, this is now a game of pure luck. He has neither a four nor a one. Everything depends on what B uses.)

A: 4-1

B: 1-0

A: 0-0

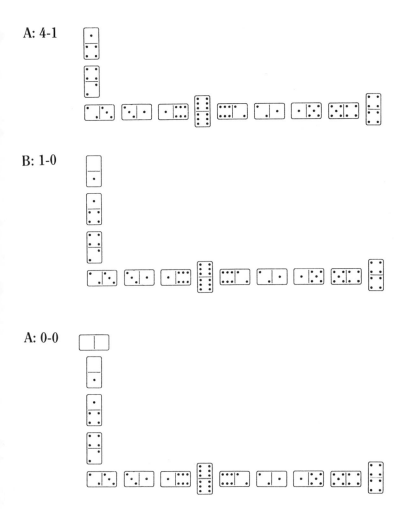

B: 5-0

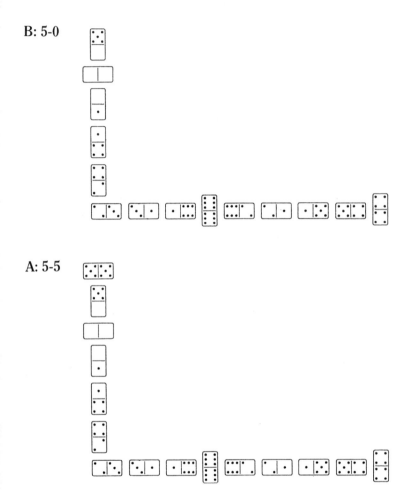

A: 5-5

(A's last tile; A wins).
Since B still has the tile 3-0, A wins 3 points, and the next game can begin.

Variations

More than two people can play this game. This short summary indicates the number of tiles per player and the size of the domino set needed.

- three players, seven tiles each, 36 tiles
- four players, six tiles each, 36 tiles
- five players, seven tiles each, 45 tiles
- six players, six tiles each, 45 tiles
- seven players, six tiles each, 55 tiles
- eight players, five tiles each, 55 tiles

Block Dominoes with Buying

The course of the game is the same as the one previously described. The only difference is that when the participants can't add on, they have to buy tiles—up to three tiles at a time.

Allies

- In this variation for four partici-

pants, Team 1 (A and B) plays against Team 2 (C and D). Each player draws a tile, and the players take turns according to the value of pips on their tiles.

Although the seating arrangement doesn't matter, it's easier if the players sit in the same order they will play in.

- In this variation, each player selects six tiles; players may not buy tiles. All other rules remain unchanged. The players are not allowed to use acoustic, optic, or other signals.
- After each game, the teams calculate their total points and determine the difference. The winning team receives the difference. For example:

Team 1
  –A: 7 pips
  –B: 5 pips
  Total 12 pips
Team 2
  –C: 0 pips
  –D: 13 pips
  Total 13 pips

Although a player on Team 2 won, this team loses the game. Team 1 gets credit for the difference, 1 point.

Blind Dominoes or Blind Hughie

You need: 28-tile set and two to four people.

- The person who draws the heaviest tile begins. The players return the tiles to the boneyard and shuffle again.
- The players now take their tiles in order, clockwise.
- The number of tiles each player picks depends on the number of players:
  - two players, eight tiles each
  - three players, seven tiles each
  - four players, six tiles each

The players do not pick any more pieces from the boneyard.

The Game

This example shows the beginning of the game with two participants, A and B.

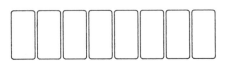

- Each player picks his tiles from the boneyard without turning

them over. Leaving them face down on the table, the player lines up his tiles in a straight row. A turns over any tile from his row.

A:

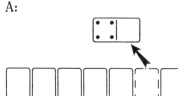

- B also takes any tile and turns it over. If this one matches the one A turned over, B adds his tile onto A's.

B:

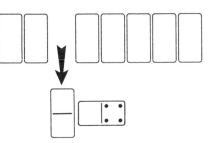

24

- If the tile does not match, then B turns it over again and places it on the left end of his row.

B:

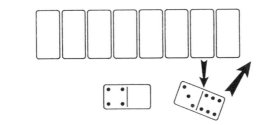

- If several people play, they take turns.
- The first one who uses all the tiles wins.
- Since the players do not take all 28 tiles, games do not always end with one person using all his tiles. Count the points in the usual way.

Tip

A player who can remember which tiles are in which position has a big advantage. Children often do very well in this game.

One Hundred Down

You need: 28-tile set and two or more players.
- Each player takes eight tiles from the boneyard. Players may buy no more than two tiles per round from the boneyard.

The Game

- The play is the same as in simple Block Dominoes. The difference is that each player starts with 100 points. The winner of a game subtracts the number of points his opponent ends up with. The object is to reduce the 100 points to zero.

Variations

When more than two people play One Hundred Down,

- the number of tiles each player receives is the same as for Block Dominoes (see page 18)
- after each game, the winner subtracts the losers' points from his number
- whoever reaches zero first wins

Here is an example:

Player B wins the first round with 18 points: A had 7 pips, and C had 11. B now has 82 points.

Thief Party

You need:

28-tile set and two teams of two players.

- Players each draw six tiles. The remaining four tiles are not part of the game.
- The four players divide into two teams. But the teams do not remain the same; they switch after three games, i.e., after a "tour."

The Game

- The game involves playing three tours, so each player plays one tour with each other player.
- The seating arrangements change for each tour so that a player of Team 1 sits next to one of Team 2.

  First Tour
  - Team 1: A and C
  - Team 2: B and D
  - Seating arrangement: A-B-C-D

  Second Tour
  - Team 1: A and B
  - Team 2: C and D
  - Seating arrangement: A-C-B-D

  Third Tour
  - Team 1: A and D

First Tour	First Game	Second Game	Third Game
Team 1: Player A	12	0	6
Player C	7	5	0
Partial Result	19	5	6
Team 2 Player B	17	8	11
Player D	0	11	2
Partial Result	17	19	13
Final Result:			
Team 1:	+17	+19	+13 : 49
Team 2:	+19	+ 5	+ 6 : 30

- Team 2: B and C
- Seating arrangement: A-B-D-C
- Determine who will be the first player by drawing lots. The other players then position their tiles, clockwise. The player with the lowest score begins each of the following games.

Domino Pool

Before the beginning of the game, the players put the same amount of money into a pool.
- The team which reaches 100 points first within a tour wins the pool. If none of the teams succeeds, then the pool remains for the following tours.

The Game

- Domino Pool uses the same rules as Block Dominoes. The players of a team score together. The winning team credits the minus points of the losing team as plus points.

- The team which reaches 100 points in a game wins double the amount of the pool.

- If a team reaches 100 points before the opponents score a single point, the team wins triple the amount in the pool.

- As soon as the contents of the pool have been won by a team, all players have to pay again.

27

Draw Dominoes

You need: 28-tile set and two or more players.
- Establish who goes first by drawing lots. The players begin the following games alternately.
- Each player draws seven tiles. The remaining tiles create the boneyard.

The Game

The rules are the same as for Block Dominoes with the following exceptions:
- If a participant cannot add on, he has to buy until he finds a matching tile.
- Players may buy all of the tiles in the boneyard, except the last two.
- In order to increase his supply, a player may buy tiles when he already owns a matching one.
- At the end of each game, the loser receives minus points for the pips on his tiles and for the pips on the two remaining tiles in the boneyard.

Closing Off

Because the players can buy any amount of tiles from the boneyard, each player has a chance to close off the game. By taking advantage of certain pip combinations which the opponent cannot have anymore, a player can force his opponent to buy tiles or to end the game because he cannot add any more tiles.

Variations

- More than two players can play Draw Dominoes.
- At the end of a game, credit the two tiles from the boneyard to the winner as plus points.
- The distribution of the tiles is as follows:
  - Three players, seven tiles each, 36 tiles
  - Four players, seven tiles each, 45 tiles
  - Five players, seven tiles each, 55 tiles

  The remaining tiles create the boneyard.

Free-Pass Dominoes

You need: 20 tiles from a 28-tile set and two or more players.

Free-Pass Dominoes is similar to Draw Dominoes, but it has an additional rule.

The Game

- The person whose turn it is may end the game by adding on a double tile. But this "free passing," which the player must announce, is a risk, since the announcement alone doesn't guarantee victory. The player who made the announcement has to win the game, otherwise he loses, and all the other players are the winners. None of the other players must be able to add on any more tiles, and none may have a lower point value than the "free-passer."

- If a free-passer loses the game, all the other participants get credit for the entire number of pips in the game, including the boneyard, as plus points.

- If the free-passer wins, he credits all the other players' points and the points of the boneyard as plus points.

Here is an example:

The game between players A and B is as follows:

- A couldn't add on and had to draw the last four tiles out of the

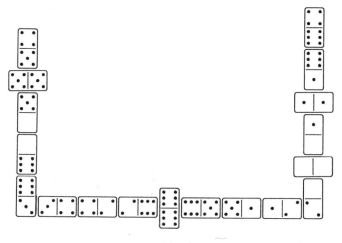

29

boneyard. He continues the game with 5-4.

- B still has three tiles, including the 4-4. He realizes now that all fours, except for the 4-1 and the two he has, are already on the table. Since A was only able to add onto the five by buying and did not add onto the 6-4, B assumes that A has no four tile.
- B adds 4-4, says, "Free-pass," and ends the game.
- Both players now turn over their tiles.

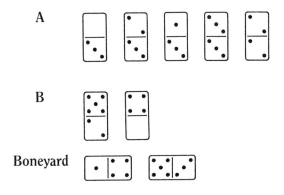

A

B

Boneyard

B has 11 pips and wins against player A's 22 pips. B gets these, as well as the 13 boneyard pips, as plus points.

30

Hungarian Dominoes

You need:
28-tile set and two to four players.
- Distribute the tiles as follows:
  - two players, twelve tiles each
  - three players, eight tiles each
  - four players, six tiles each

  The remaining tiles aren't part of the game.
- The player with the heaviest tile begins; the others follow, clockwise.

The Game

- The rules are the same as for Block Dominoes.
- The first player lays down his tile and then adds on any more that match. Then the next player uses as many tiles as possible and so on and so on.
- When nobody can add on any more pieces, the game ends, and each player counts his remaining pips.
- The loser is the first person to have 100 points.

31

In the following games, you will learn new ways to add on tiles. Players use tiles in order to score a lot of points.

Italian Dominoes

You need: 28-tile set and three to five players.

- Distribute the tiles as follows:
  - three players, seven tiles each
  - four players, four tiles each
  - five players, four tiles each

  The remaining tiles become the boneyard.
- Each player may buy only one tile per round. A player who buys may not add on in that round.
- The player with the heaviest tile begins the game; the others follow, clockwise.
- These are the numbers and points:
  - 30 pips: 1 point
  - 50 pips: 2 points
  - 70 pips: 4 points
  - 100 pips: 8 points
- The players determine how many games they want to play.

The Game

- The first player places the heavi-est tile and names the pip number.
- Every player plays any tile (!) he wants, adding the pip number to the previous one and naming the sum (A: 6–6 = 12, B: 5–3 = 20, C: 0-0 = 20). Players try to reach the winning sum with one of their own tiles in order to receive the points.
- If a player misses a winning sum, for example, a player reaches 32 instead of 30 pips, then no other player receives that winning point. The game continues, and players try to reach the other points.

Matador

You need: 28-tile set and two to four players.
- Distribute the tiles as follows:
  - two players, eight tiles each
  - three players, six tiles each
  - four players, five tiles each

  The remaining tiles create the boneyard.
- Each player may take a maximum of one tile per round from the boneyard.
- The player with the highest double begins.

32

The Game

The special attraction of Matador
is the way players add tiles.

- The pip numbers of the adjacent
  squares must always result in 7.
- Except for 0-0, players add doubles lengthwise and not crosswise.
- Matador tiles have pip totals of
  7, except for 0-0, which also
  counts as a Matador.

- Players may add Matadors on
  each free end. In fact, these tiles
  function as jokers. The player
  decides which square to add a
  Matador to.

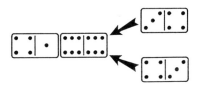

- Adding on a Matador is the only
  way to continue the game at a
  free end which shows a blank,
  or zero.

33

- If a player adds a Matador crosswise, then at this end the game continues with the same number of pips as on the square before the Matador.

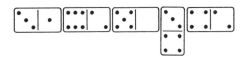

- If a player places a Matador so that only one square of the tile lies in the domino row, then the number of pips of the square below the row becomes the number to continue the game.

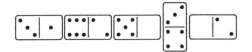

- If a player adds a Matador crosswise, it is up to the following player to decide which of the two numbers he wants to use to continue the game.

Variations

- Players can use a 55-tile set to play Matador. Then, all tiles with pips that add up to 10 are Matadors.
- In order to add on a tile, the pips of the squares next to each other must add up to 10.

34

Cross Dominoes

You need:
28-tile set and four players.

- Each player draws six tiles.
- The remaining tiles are not part of the game.
- The game begins with the highest double.
- The first player immediately adds another tile, or he passes.
- The other players continue the game clockwise.

The Game

- In the first round, each player has to add onto the double tile. Anyone who can't has to pass.
- After the first round, the usual rules apply. Every player may add on at one of the four free ends.
- If fewer than four free ends are available, players only add onto these, not onto the first tile.

Here is an example:

The first tile was the 5-5. One of the players wasn't able to add on, so there are only three free ends: 6, 4, and 1.

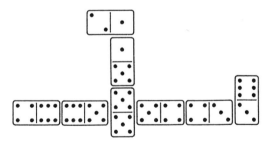

Sebastopol

You need: 28-tile set and four players.

- Each player draws seven tiles, and there is no boneyard.
- Whoever owns 6-6 opens with this piece.

The Game

- The first player immediately adds on another tile, or he has to pass. The other players take their turns clockwise.
- In the first round, each player has to add onto one of the four free ends of the double tile. Anyone who can't do that passes.
- From the second round on, the usual rules apply—each player adds a matching tile onto one of the four free ends.

Here is an example:

Of the four free ends, two already have tiles added on.

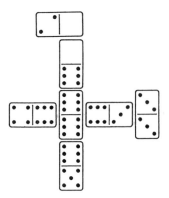

Cyprus

You need: 55-tile set and four to eight players.

36

- Distribute the tiles as follows:
  - four players, nine tiles each
  - five players, eight tiles each
  - six players, seven tiles each
  - seven players, six tiles each
  - eight players, five tiles each

  The remaining tiles create the boneyard.
- Players may buy only one tile per round.
- Whoever owns 9-9 opens the game. If it isn't in the game, everyone buys a tile, until 9-9 appears.

The Game

- Players add nine tiles to the 9-9 in the first round. They place the tiles in eight directions. Anyone who can't do that has to buy a tile. If that tile doesn't match, the player loses his turn.

- In the second round, the game continues according to the usual rules, with every player adding a matching tile onto one of the free ends.

Maltese Cross

You need: 28-tile set and two to four players.

- Distribute the tiles as follows:
  - two players, seven tiles each
  - three or four players, five tiles each

  The remaining tiles create the boneyard.
- Every player may buy one tile per round from the boneyard.
- The person who has the heaviest double opens the game.

The Game

- If there are four participants, the players add their tiles onto the double in four directions in the first round. If there are two players, they accomplish this in two rounds (see illustration, top of page 38). Anyone who cannot add on passes.

- First round.

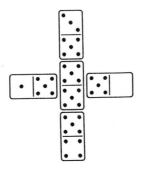

- In the second round, players may only use doubles. They place these crosswise. Players may not use normal tiles unless the matching double is already on the table.

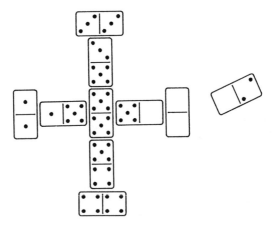

- For the third round, one square of each tile has to have the following number of pips: 0, 1, 2, 3, or 4.

- From the fourth round on, the players add on tiles according to the usual rules of Block Dominoes.

All Fives

You need: 28-tile set and two to four players.

- Players draw lots to decide who will play first. Then each player draws five tiles.
- The first player opens with any tile.
- If it is a double tile, the players can continue in four directions.

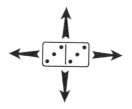

The Game

- If the first tile isn't a double, but a normal tile, then the game continues in two directions.

- The game switches to four directions as soon as a player uses a double.

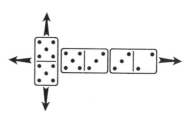

- The number five and multiples of it (10, 15, 20 . . .) are the basis of the points in this game. The goal of the game is to reach exactly 61 points.
- Players receive points for winning a game—the pips of the loser count as plus points for the winner. They also earn points during a game when they succeed in reaching the number five or a multiple of it by adding on a tile. Every player who adds on a tile counts the pips on the squares of the free ends.

Examples of points are on page 40.

Total 5: 1 point

Total 10: 2 points

Total 15: 3 points

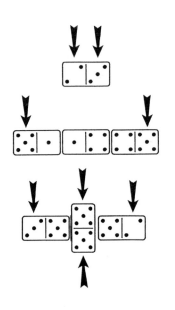

Total 20: 4 points

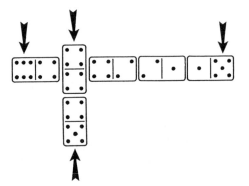

A opens with 5-0 and receives 1 point.

B uses 5-5 and receives 2 points: 5 + 5 = 10.

A continues the game with the 6-0, but earns no points.

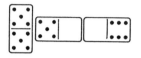

- A player may also subtract the number of pips at the free end of a tile in order to obtain a favorable result.

B lays down 5-1 and earns the total from all three free end-points:

5 + 5 + 6 − 1 = 15.

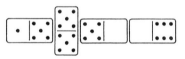

Whoever reaches exactly 61 points first wins the game. When a player exceeds that number, the last points that were earned expire, and the game continues.

- If a player has 57 points and would earn another 11 points from the victory of the game, the player doesn't count these points, and the game continues.

Variations

Without changing the rules, players can use another evaluation system which will end the game faster.

- The winner is the first to reach 150, 200 points, or more.
- The points assigned to the winner are the same as above.
- Players also receive points during the game. Players who produce the number five or a multiple of it receive 1 point for each pip on free-end tiles.

In the following example, the player receives 20 points from the number of pips on the four free ends.

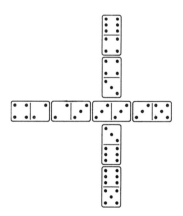

41

All Threes

You need: 28-tile set and two to four players.

The Game

The game is similar to All Fives, but as the title indicates, the point is to reach the number three or a multiple of it on the free ends.
- Total 3: 1 point
- Total 6: 2 points
- Total 9: 3 points
- Total 12: 4 points

Variations

You can combine All Fives and All Threes.
- The five and the three are worth points.

A player receives:
- 1 point per pip when the end total results in a three (or a multiple of it) OR a five (or a multiple of it).

End total: 6   Points: 6

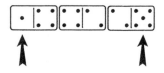

- 2 points per pip when the end total results in a multiple of three AND five.

End total: 15

Points: 30 (3 and 5 contained in it)

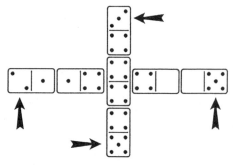

- The winner of a game also receives one point for each pip his opponent still holds.

Bergen

You need: 28-tile set and two to four players.

- Distribute the tiles as follows:
  - two or three players, six tiles each
  - four players, five tiles each

  The remaining tiles create the boneyard, or the players agree that they have to pass if they cannot add on.
- If buying is permitted, players may only buy one tile per round.
- The player with the heaviest double begins. The other players follow, clockwise.
- The participants determine how many games they want to play or the number of points (10 or 15 points) it takes to win a game.

The Game

- The usual rules apply: The players add matching tiles onto the two free ends.

- A player who cannot or does not want to add on may buy a tile. If there is no buying, the player must pass.
- Players score:
  - 2 points when the two free ends have the same numbers of pips and for opening with a double

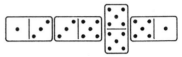

  - 3 points when the same number of pips occurs on three free ends (one of the tiles, therefore, has to be a double)

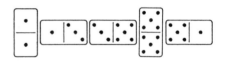

  - 2 points for winning a game
- If a game ends blocked, then the winning player is the one who
  - does not hold a double tile
  OR
  - has the fewest double tiles
  OR
  - has the fewest pips

43

Here's an example:
A: 6-6 = 2 points

B: 6-3 = 0 points

A: 6-4 = 0 points

B: 4-3 = 2 points

A: 3-3 = 3 points

B: 3-0 = 0 points

A: 0-1 = 0 points

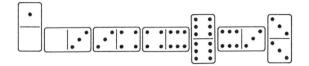

B: 1-3 = 3 points

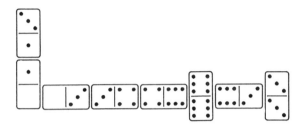

After four moves, A and B cannot add any more, since they have decided to pass rather than buy. The score is 5-all.

A still holds tiles 4-2 and 5-1 (12 points), and B has tiles 6-0 and 5-2 (13 points). A gets credit for the one point difference.

The following games have very little in common with those previously described. These games involve modifications of other types of games, giving them a completely different appeal.

Forty-Two

You need: 28-tile set and four players divided into two teams.

- Forty-Two resembles a card game in which the players bid first. After that, the goal is to take tricks. The number bid has to be reached with the pips of the dominoes.
- Every player receives seven tiles.
- A match consists of several games, ending when a team reaches 250 points.
- Every game consists of seven rounds, or tricks.

Classification by Points

- The first player plays a tile. The other participants each play a tile, one after another.
- The tile with the highest value wins the trick and takes the four tiles. Players receive one point for winning a trick.
- Players win additional points for special tiles. The player who wins a trick with a special tile receives the points.
- Tiles with 5 pips are worth 5 points. They are the 5-0, 4-1, and 3-2 tiles.

The two tiles showing 10 pips are worth 10 points. These are the 6-4 and the 5-5.

- In each round of a game, players can win a total of 42 points. The illustration shows three example tricks with their point valuations.

1 point

6 points (5 + 1)

11 points (10 + 1)

- This game also has trumps. Each of the six numbers and the blank can be trump. The highest tile is the double. The remaining values follow in descending order.

  In the following example, the three is trump, the highest tile is the double, 3-3, then the:

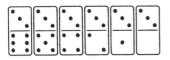

- A player may also declare the double tiles as trumps. The highest is 6-6. Then come the 5-5, 4-4, 3-3, 2-2, 1-1, and 0-0.
- A player may also decide to play a game without trumps.

The Game

- A player shuffles the tiles. The player on his left draws seven tiles; the others follow, clockwise. The succession of the shuffling for the following rounds is also clockwise.
- The two players on a team sit opposite each other.
- The player who has drawn his tiles first is the first one to bid. He names a number, or he passes. Then the other players bid.
- When a player bids, he is pledging the number of points that he believes he and his partner can earn by taking tricks, or rounds.

- The minimum bid is 30 pips, but players may bid any number between 30 and 42.
- If a player bids 42 pips, the next player can only double to 84 or pass. The third participant has to double again, to 168, or pass. The same is true for the last player, to 250.
- Anyone who bids 42 must win all 42 points, or he loses.
- The winner receives all the points (42, 84, 168, or 250).
- The player with the highest bid determines which pip is trump or whether to play the game without trumps. This player also opens the game.
- The highest number of pips of the first-played tile is the round number (like the suit in a card game). All players must play this number. Anyone who cannot do so may trump in a game with trumps. In a game without trumps, the player has to discard any tile.

Here's an example:

A, who made the highest bid, decides to play without trumps. He opens with 6-5. In this first round, the six becomes the round number. This means that all other participants must follow with a six tile. Anyone who cannot do this discards a tile.

- The values of the game number correspond to those of the trumps. For example, the highest five, 5-5, is the highest tile. Then come 5-6, 5-4, 5-3, 5-2, 5-1, and 5-0.
- If a player makes a trick in a round, he is the first one to play a tile in the next round.
- Each game ends after seven tricks, and the points are totaled. When the team with the highest bid reaches the number it bid, it also receives the number of points it bid.
- If the team fails to reach its bid, the opponents receive the points of the bid and the points from their own tricks.
- The game ends when one team reaches 250 points.

A and C form one team; B and D form the other one.

- A bids 30 pips. He has two special tiles with 5 points each; his trump would be the blank, or zero.
- B passes.
- C bids 38 pips. He has a special tile with 10 points; his trump would be the three.
- D bids 40 pips. He has two special tiles totaling 15 points. He declares the five as trump and opens the game.

The following pages show an example game.

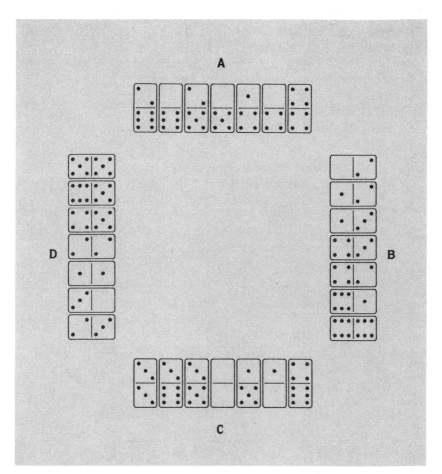

First Round

- D has the three highest trumps, and he plays one of them. Except for B, all the others have to follow suit with a trump.

- D: 5-4
- A: 5-2
- B: 6-1
- C: 5-1
- D wins the trick and earns 1 point.

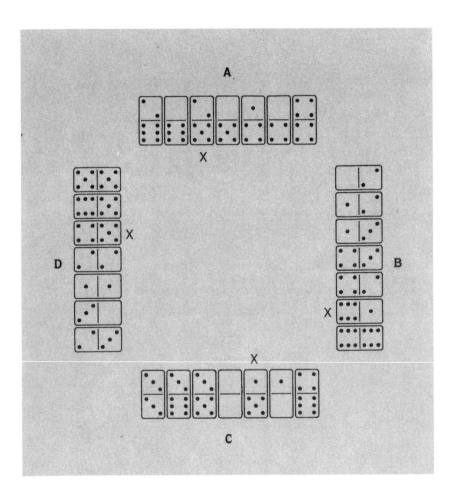

Second Round

D again plays a trump. A now has to play his special tile worth 5 points.

- D: 5-6
- A: 5-0
- B: 0-2
- C: 5-3
- D wins the trick and scores 6 points.

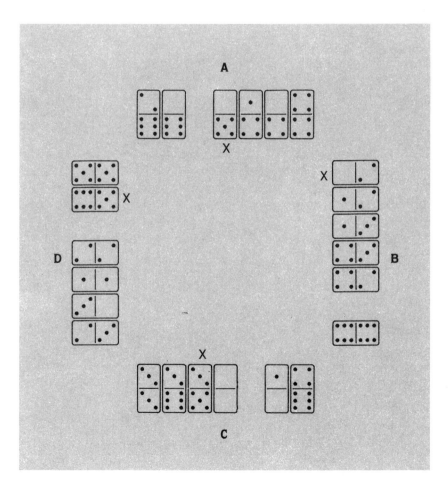

51

Third Round

D leads with his special 10-point tile.

- D: 5-5
- A: 4-0
- B: 2-1
- C: 1-0
- D wins the trick and earns 11 points.

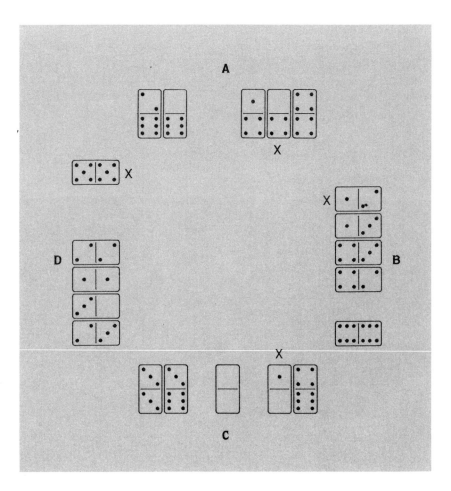

Fourth Round

D plays the highest tile of the round, number one. Anyone who can has to follow, even A with his special 5-point tile.

- D: 1-5
- A: 1-4
- B: 1-3
- C: 3-6
- D takes the trick and scores 6 points.

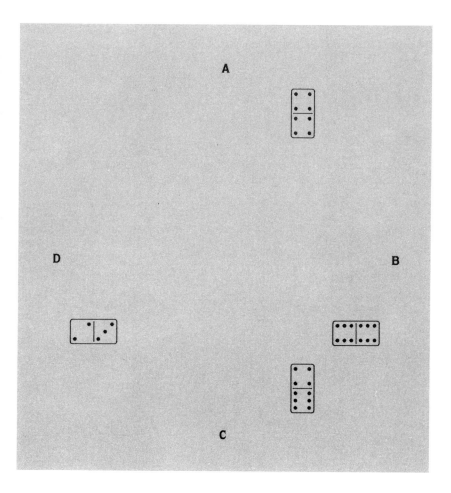

Fifth Round

D opens this round with the highest tile of the round, number two. C has to consider which tile to discard. He wants to keep his special tile under any circumstances.

- D: 2-2
- A: 6-2
- B: 4-2
- C: 0-0
- D wins the trick and 1 point.

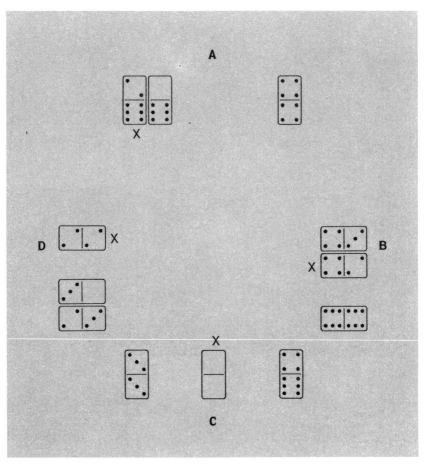

Sixth Round

D opens again, but he holds onto his special tile.

- D: 3-0
- A: 6-0
- B: 3-4
- C: 3-3
- C wins the trick and receives 1 point.

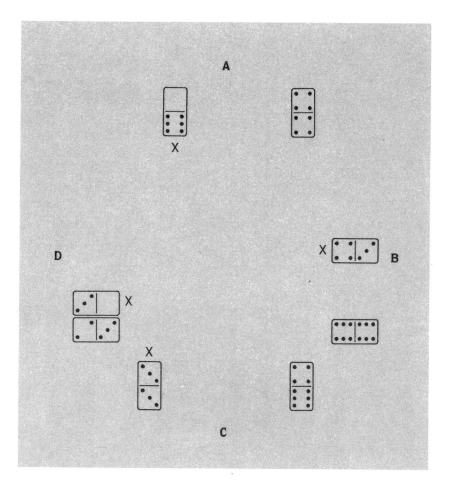

55

Seventh Round

C plays his 10-point tile, and D has to play his 5-point tile.

- C: 6-4
- D: 3-2
- A: 4-4
- B: 6-6
- B wins the trick and 16 points. The team of B and D has 41 points. The bid was only 40.

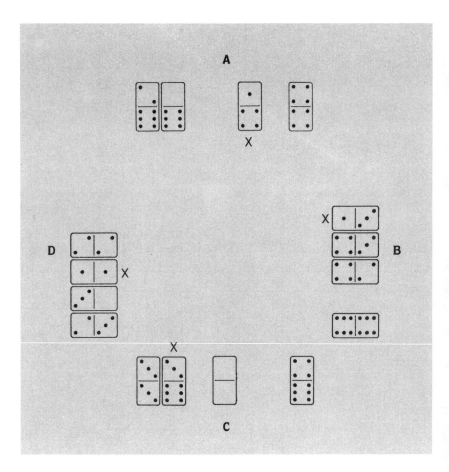

Bingo

You need: 28-tile set and two players.

- Bingo is a card game altered for domino tiles. The object is to win seven sets.
- After shuffling, A draws a tile, face down. B has to guess whether the number of pips is odd or even. If he is right, he goes first; if he guesses wrong, A opens the game.
- A puts the tile back, and they shuffle the tiles one more time. The first player takes seven tiles, and then the second player takes seven tiles.
- The remaining tiles create the boneyard.
- To determine trump, the first player uncovers one of the tiles from the boneyard. The higher of the two pip squares determines the trump number. That tile remains open.
- In order to win a set, a player has to reach 70 points. The number of games needed to reach 70 points depends on luck.

The Game

- The first player, here A, places any tile face up. Then it's B's turn.

  In Bingo, the second player may play any tile he wants. He doesn't have to follow suit or play trump. That holds true until a player "closes" the game by turning over the trump tile, which is lying face up.

- The player who wins a trick is the first to draw another tile from the boneyard. He may play any tile he likes for the next trick.
- If there are only two tiles left in the boneyard (the trump tile, which is face up or down, and another tile, face down), then the winner of the last trick takes the trump tile and his opponent gets the last tile.
- 0-0, "Bingo," beats any other tile, including the double trump.
- If both players play trumps, the higher one wins.
- Except for 0-0, trump tiles beat other tiles.

- In the case of two tiles that are not trumps, the tile with the higher total pip number takes the trick: 6-5 beats 5-5 (11 to 10) and 4-4 beats 6-1 (8 to 7).
- If there are no trumps on the trick and both tiles have the same number of pips, then the player who played first wins the trick.

Value of the Tricks

- Some tiles have a special value:

10 points

10 points

14 points

- A zero, or blank, square counts as 7 points; therefore, the Bingo (0-0) is worth 14 points.
- The double of the trump number always counts as 28 points.
- Doubles that are not trump are worth their total number of pips.

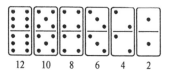

12   10   8   6   4   2

- The values of the other trump tiles correspond to the number of their pips.

The blank square counts as 7 points. Here is a listing of the individual trump numbers:

SIX

- = 28
- = 11
- = 10
- = 9
- = 8
- = 7
- = 13

FIVE

- = 28
- = 11
- = 9
- = 8
- = 7
- = 6
- = 12

FOUR

- = 28
- = 10
- = 9
- = 7
- = 6
- = 5
- = 11

THREE

- = 28
- = 9
- = 8
- = 7
- = 5
- = 4
- = 10

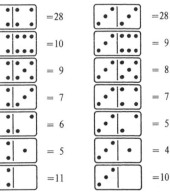

TWO

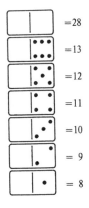

	=28
	= 8
	= 7
	= 6
	= 5
	= 3
	= 9

ONE

	=28
	= 7
	= 6
	= 5
	= 4
	= 3
	= 8

BLANK

	=28
	=13
	=12
	=11
	=10
	= 9
	= 8

Point Distribution

Because the value of a tile changes according to the trump number, different totals are possible in different games. To get these different totals, players add trumps, doubles, and special tiles. Here are the totals for each trump number:

Six: 140 points (86 + 44 + 10)
Five: 147 points (81 + 46 + 20)
Four: 144 points (76 + 48 + 20)
Three: 131 points (71 + 50 + 10)
Two: 138 points (66 + 52 + 20)
One: 135 points (61 + 54 + 20)
Zero: 143 points (91 + 42 + 10)

- Participants receive additional points when they have two or more double tiles.
- To receive the points, a player must announce that he has them when it is his turn and when he makes the trick.
- If a player has two doubles, he receives 20 points when he:
  - places **one** of them
  - shows the second one
  - announces **double**

If a player has more than two doubles, he can earn more points, again by using one, showing the other one, and winning tricks. If a player has:
- three doubles, 40 points
- four doubles, 50 points
- five doubles, **King**, 60 points
- six doubles, **Emperor**, 70 points
- **Bingo**, additional 10 points
- seven doubles, **Invincible**, 210 points
- Write down the points a player receives per trick immediately.

Closing a Game

- When a participant believes that he will have the necessary 70 points without having to draw more tiles from the boneyard, he closes the game by turning over the trump tile which was lying face up.
- Once a player closes the game, neither player may draw tiles from the boneyard.
- As soon as a player closes a game or when the boneyard is empty,

both participants have to play numbers.
- If a player uses a trump, the opponent must play trump. If he does not have one, he discards any tile.
- If a player uses a tile that is not trump, the higher pip number of a square is the round number. If the opponent cannot play this, then the lower pip number is the round number.

Round Numbers

Round Numbers, if he does not have a five

- If the opponent can play none of the pip numbers, then he has to make a trick with a trump. If he does not have one, he has to discard a tile.

Scoring

- The winner gets one set for every 70 points (from tricks or

60

doubles) if the game went until the end.

- A player earns a set if he scores 70 points, while his opponent scores at least 30 points.
- A player receives two sets if he scores 70 points, while his opponent scores less than 30.
- A player who reaches 70 points before his opponent scores at all earns three sets.
- A player who wins the double trump with the Bingo wins a set.
- However, in order to earn points and sets, a player has to announce them.

Ending the Game

- A game consists of seven sets. A player must have 70 points to win.
- A game ends when all the tiles have been played.
- To score, each player adds up the points he has reached during the game.

You can play different types of dominoes by yourself. Exercise your mind with solitaire games. You can spend hours entertaining yourself with your domino set. You need a set with 28 tiles.

Magical Squares

For Magical Squares with domino tiles, you will need to spend more time thinking than calculating.

The Game

- Spread out the domino tiles face up in front of you.
- Take nine tiles. Arrange the tiles in three rows of three tiles so that the sum of the pips of three tiles in a row always results in the same number vertically, horizontally, and diagonally. To do this, you have to solve two problems for each of the three magical squares:
  - Which tiles should you choose?
  - How should you arrange the tiles?

- You'll find the solutions on page 90).

Sum 12

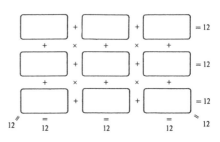

Sum 15

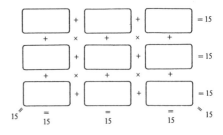

Sum 18

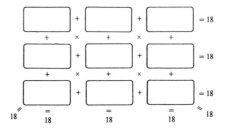

If you enjoy such tasks, maybe you can think of others with different sums.

Devilish Square

The Game

This game presents a similar problem to be solved. The object is to arrange 16 tiles in four rectangles, so that each sum results in 18. In addition, the rows of all rectangles (vertical, horizontal, and diagonal) also must result in the sum of 18. You'll find the solution on page 90.

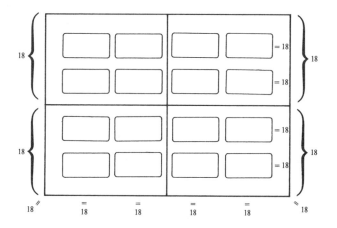

Blasted 21

The Game

The following four variations use the 28 tiles of a domino game arranged in the illustrated forma- tion. In each formation, each row (horizontal and vertical) ends up with the sum of 21 when you add up the numbers of pips. That holds true for the shorter rows at the edge!

You'll find the solutions on page 91.

First Task

The illustration gives you the position of nine tiles, and you must find out all the others for yourself.

Second Task

The illustration gives you the position of ten tiles. In order to make it a little harder for you, symbols replace the numbers of the pips. The same symbol stands for the same number of pips.

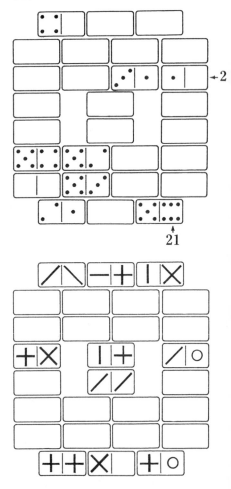

Third Task

Here, the illustration only shows the positions of squares, not of the entire tiles.

Fourth Task

Here, the illustration shows only the positions of the double tiles.

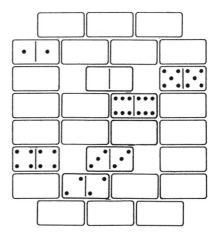

Chaos on the Square

The Game

The following two tasks show the 28 tiles of a domino set. However, instead of the usual pips, you'll find numbers. The edge lines of the individual tiles are missing. You have to find out these to determine the position of the tiles.

Tip

The first task is much easier than the second task, where everything is a jumble.

You'll find the solutions on page 92.

First Task

5	1	4	0	2	6	0
1	6	3	0	4	0	4
4	2	2	4	6	2	3
6	5	2	1	5	6	2
1	5	3	6	1	1	0
3	0	3	6	2	1	1
4	2	5	3	5	5	3
4	0	3	6	5	4	0

Second Task

3	5	1	1	3	4	4
3	3	6	4	3	1	4
2	5	1	0	0	1	1
1	3	0	0	0	4	4
1	6	0	0	0	5	2
6	6	6	5	2	6	3
6	6	5	5	2	2	2
4	3	4	5	5	2	2

Pushings

The Game

- Pick out the tiles you need and place them on a piece of cardboard in exactly the same position as in the illustration. Draw a frame to serve as a border. The tiles must stay within the border.
- The task is easy to describe: Move 0-0 (in the second task: 1-1) from the lower left-hand corner to the free space in the upper right-hand corner. To do so, you keep moving or pushing tiles into the free space.
- The pip number of the last tile moved may not border the same pip number of another square.
- At the end, the free space has to be on the lower left, where the 0-0 began.

Tip

With your first move, push 3-1 upwards. For your second move, you must not push 4-1 to the right, since otherwise two squares with the same pip number would be next to each other.

No solutions are given in Solutions, but rest assured that both tasks take less than 100 moves.

First Pushing

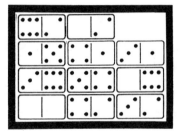

Second Pushing

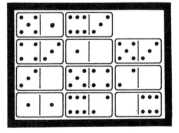

Fraction Dominoes

The Game

- Put all doubles and all tiles with blanks aside.
- Arrange the remaining 15 tiles in three rows of 5 tiles each.
- Consider each tile as a fraction. You can use both proper and improper fractions.

First Task

Arrange all the tiles in each row so that the sum is always 4.

Second Task

The sum should be 10 in each row.
   You'll find the solutions on page 93.

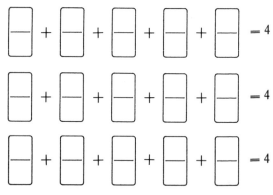

68

Multiplications

The illustration shows a simple multiplication task. Every game uses four tiles. The example is $540 \times 3 = 1620$.

The Game

From your 28-tile set, create as many multiplications as possible. With one complete set, you can work on seven at a time.

You'll find the solutions on page 93.

Seven Squares

The Game

Using all 28 tiles, create seven squares with four tiles each. Each of the four sides of a square must have the same pip number. The number will be different in five squares, but the number will be the same in two of the squares.

You'll find the solution on page 92.

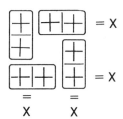

Domino Labyrinth

The object of Domino Labyrinth is to create a path from the upper left-hand square to the bottom right-hand square.

The Game

Place your pencil on the tile in the upper left-hand corner. The pip (one) indicates how many squares you may move in a straight line. Here, you may move one square. The pip number you've landed on determines the number of squares of your next move. Eventually you reach the square in the lower right-hand corner. You'll find the solutions on page 94.

In the following example you must travel in three straight moves horizontally and vertically from the upper left-hand one square to the blank square in the bottom right-hand corner.

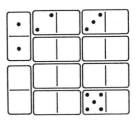

The first move begins on the one square and brings you one square to the right. In the second move, you may move two more squares because the pip number is 2. In the third move, the pip number 3 allows you to move three squares.

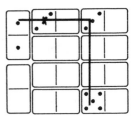

70

First Labyrinth

Begin on the one square in the top left-hand corner. Moving in horizontal and vertical directions, use exactly eight steps to reach the six square in the bottom right-hand corner.

Second Labyrinth

Moving in a straight direction, horizontally or vertically, start on the one square in the top left-hand corner and finish on the six square in the bottom right-hand corner. The sum of the pips of the squares you land on (retraced moves and starting and ending squares do not count) must result in 18 when divided by three.

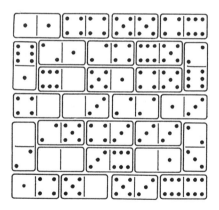

Third Labyrinth

Begin on one of the one squares in the top left. In five diagonal steps, move onto one of the two five squares in the bottom right.

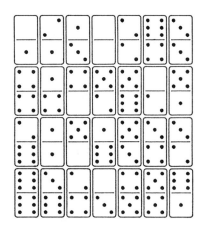

Fourth Labyrinth

Begin on the blank square in the top left-hand corner. Move to the square in the bottom right-hand corner. Use horizontal as well as vertical directions. On your way, you must enter the following 15 square values, including the starting and ending tiles. The sequence of the moves is up to you.

Square values: 1, 1, 1, 2, 2, 3, 3, 4, 4, 5, 5, 6, 6, 0, 0.

You might be a little surprised that you can play solitaire with domino tiles. In this version, the tiles are face down. You turn them over and place them on top of each other or next to each other, depending on the rule, in the correct order, so that they are all face up at the end. Like most solitaire games, you play Domino Solitaire against yourself. For the following two games, you'll need 28-tile sets.

Little Harp

- Shuffle the 28 tiles face down, then create the formation below.

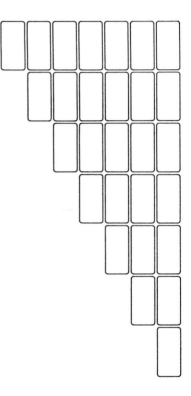

- Uncover the bottom tile in each of the seven vertical rows.

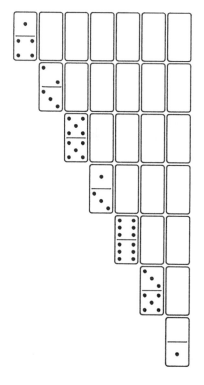

- In the case of the domino tiles, each one, except for the doubles, has two different pip numbers.

- Turn over a tile so that the square that was the bottom one before becomes the top one.

The Game

- Place the uncovered tiles which have the same number of pips next to each other. However, you can't turn the tiles in the matching direction!
- You may uncover tiles that have become free.
- If one of the seven vertical rows becomes free, you may place tiles that do not fit into your own row in the upper horizontal row, including doubles.

For example, the following tiles are lying in one row underneath each other:

Tile 1 (on top): face down
Tile 2: 0-5
Tile 3: 2-1
Tile 4: 1-3
Tile 5: 3-4

Even though tiles 3, 4, and 5 go together, they do not go with tile 2. You may place them on top.

Here are nine moves of a game of Little Harp.

First Move

Uncover the first row. You can add on four tiles.

Second Move

Four uncovered tiles have become free. In the following moves, it makes sense to free up rows.

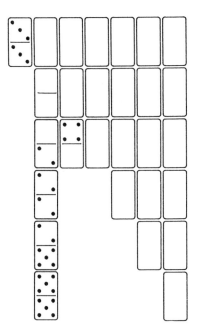

75

Third Move

Three of the uncovered tiles match.

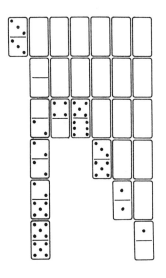

Fourth Move

You can only add on three different values.

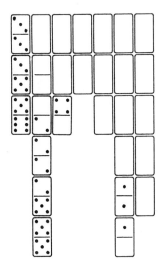

Fifth Move

Only two tiles match.

Sixth Move

You have four possibilities to add on, and you may uncover two tiles.

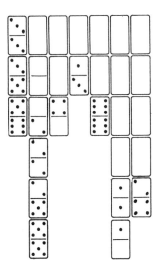

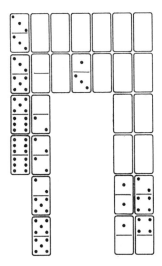

Seventh Move

All three tiles fit below each other in the second row.

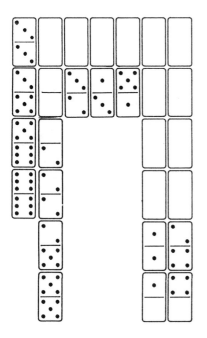

Eighth Move

You have freed up three tiles, and you have three possibilities to add on.

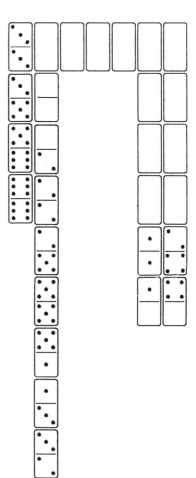

Ninth Move

You can add on the 4-6. This way, a space in the upper column becomes free.

For the tenth move, it makes sense to place 1-1 with 1-0 in the empty row so that you can uncover a tile. If you place 6-6 on top or move the next row from 5-5 on, the game will be lost immediately.

Triangle

The Game

- Remove all tiles with a blank from a 28-tile set.
- Mix the remaining 21 tiles and arrange them face down in the pattern illustrated.

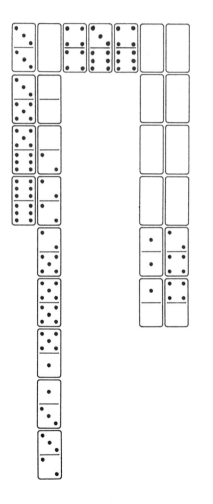

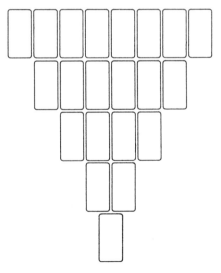

- Begin by uncovering the edge tiles.
- It is up to you to decide whether to do this as in Little Harp, from the bottom up, or equally on the two sides.

- In every vertical row, you may turn over one tile (eight altogether) to make a match. In this example, it is 5-3, in order to add 3-3 to it.

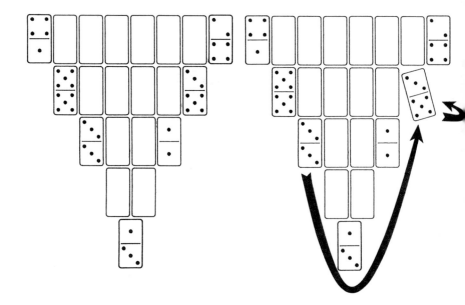

Dominoes is only suitable for children after they develop a feeling for number values and can understand the different numbers of the pips. Before you introduce children to Block Dominoes, try the following games first.

Running Dominoes

You need: 28-tile set, 6 playing figures or men, 1 die, and two to six players.

The Game

- Each player throws the die once. He may move his man one square if the square has the same pip number as the number on the die.
- A man may move in a straight line or diagonally.
- Blank squares count as jokers. A man may move onto an adjacent joker regardless of the number on the die.

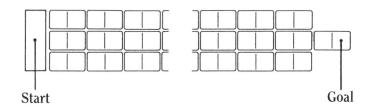

Start   Goal

- Running Dominoes is a simple racing game. The object is to be the first to reach the goal square.
- Form a triple row, nine tiles long, with the shuffled dominoes. The tiles should be face down. The 28th tile is the goal.
- Turn the tiles over.
- Each player places his man at the start of the game.
- The first player rolls the die, and the game begins.

- Since everyone likes to take advantage of moving onto jokers, they can be dangerous squares because any man occupying a square on which another man lands has to return to the starting position.
  Here's an example:
- A opens the game. He throws a three with the die and may not move his man.
- Since B has thrown a two with the die, he moves his figure

81

from the start diagonally onto the 2 square.

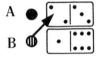

- A, in the meantime, is on 5 and throws a two with the die. He may move his man onto 2 or onto the blank, which counts as a joker.

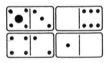

- The first player to reach the goal square wins the game.

Domino Lotto

You need: 28-tile set and two to seven players.

Material: Sixes dominoes (28 tiles).

- The object of the game is to collect as many tiles as possible with a certain pip number.
- Every player chooses a pip number and announces the number to the other players.
- Place the shuffled tiles in a block of four rows with seven tiles in each.

The Game

- Uncover all the tiles for two minutes, and then turn them over again. The players have to remember the position of the tiles with their pip number.
- In order to make the game a little more difficult, the players now rotate one seat clockwise.
- The youngest player begins by taking a tile which he shows to the others. If the tile has the correct pip number (the one he

chose), he keeps it. If it is the wrong tile, he puts it back face down. Then the next player takes a turn.

Here's an example:

- A chose the five. He picks up 5-5 and keeps the tile.
- B, who chose the blank, picks 3-2. He shows it to everyone and puts it back, face down.
- Now it's easy for C, who chose three. He takes the 3-2.
- The game ends as soon as a player collects four tiles with his pip number.

Dice Dominoes

You need: 28-tile set, two dice, and two to six players.

- In this game, a player throws the dice and has to get the combinations of a domino tile in order to receive it.
- Arrange all 28 tiles face up in a block of four rows with seven tiles each.

- The player who rolls the highest with the dice begins the game. The other players follow, clockwise.

The Game

- The players play with two dice to reach the values of a domino tile. If they are successful, they may take the tile. Then the next player takes his turn.
- If a player throws a six, he may also count it as a zero or blank.
- If a player rolls only one of the numbers on a tile, he gets a second try with one die. If this succeeds, he takes the tile. If it fails, the tile remains, and it is the next player's turn.
- Players who can't take tiles pass the dice to the next player. Towards the end of the game, this happens rather frequently, because there are only a few tiles available.

You'll find an example on page 84.

- A throws a four and a five and takes 4-5.

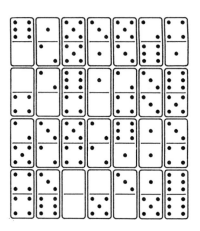

- B throws a six and a one. The 6-1 is not there anymore, but 0-1 is. Since B can also count the six as a zero, he takes this tile.
- C throws a three and a two. The three counts towards the 3-3. In the second try, he throws a six, and he can't take any tile.

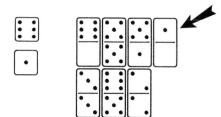

- Players determine the end of the game by setting a time limit, or by agreeing on a certain number of tiles that have to be collected. For example, in the case of
  - two players, thirteen tiles
  - three players, nine tiles
  - four players, seven tiles
  - five players, six tiles
  - six players, five tiles

The players can also decide to end the game by pip score.

For example,
- two players, 170 pips
- three to four players, 50 pips
- five to six players, 30 pips

Collecting Dominoes

You need: 28-tile set and two to four players.

The object is to collect as many tiles as possible that have the same value.

- Shuffle the tiles, place them face down on the table, and arrange them in a square with seven tiles on a side.
- The youngest player begins by removing three consecutive tiles from the square. He sets these up in front of him so that no one else can see their values.
- The second player takes the next three tiles and the other players follow in the same way.

The Game

- A takes another tile. He has a choice. He can keep this tile, or he can place it face up in the middle of the square. Remember, the goal is to collect as many tiles as possible with the same value.
- B has to decide whether he wants to take the tile A left in the middle. If not, he chooses one out of the square. B may keep it or discard it.

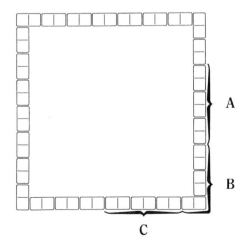

- If the last player does not take the tile that the first player placed in the middle, the tile is considered lost and may not be used by anyone.
- The game ends when the players have used all the tiles in the square.

Scoring

- Then every player turns over his collected tiles.
- Players receive points for tiles with the same pip numbers. For example,
  - two of the same, 2 points each
  - three of the same, 6 points each
  - four of the same, 6 points each
  - five of the same, 8 points each
  - any additional one of the same, 10 points each
- Players lose points for tiles that do not match:
  - one, 1 point
  - two, 3 points
  - any additional ones, 5 points each
- Whoever has the most points wins the game.

Here's an example for a player who has collected eight tiles:

5-1, 5-3, 5-5: 12 points (4 + 4 + 4)

4-3, 4-2: 4 points (2 + 2)

1-2, 1-6: 4 points (2 + 2)

3-3:   -1 point

Total = 19 points

Picture Dominoes for Small Children

From about the age of four years, Picture Dominoes is an ideal game. Toy stores offer them with many different motifs, but your family can make one that will be something special.

You'll need 28 wooden rectangles or cardboard cards $2\frac{1}{4} \times 4\frac{3}{4}$ inches (6 × 12 cm) or $3\frac{1}{2} \times 3\frac{1}{8}$ inches (9 × 8 cm) and $\frac{3}{8}$ to $\frac{5}{8}$ inch (1 to $1\frac{1}{2}$ cm) thick, photos or drawings, glue, and clear varnish or transparent tape.

If you make wooden tiles, be sure to smooth them with sandpaper. Of course, it's easier just to make the tiles from cardboard.

The Motifs

The 28-tile set on the right uses neutral symbols for seven different values. You can add color by painting the crosses in red, the circles in blue, the dots in violet, and so on.

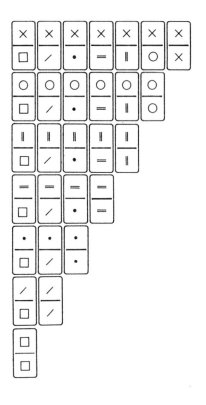

87

If you want to craft your family's own domino game, you can use special motifs.

For example:
- the members of your family
- your children's friends
- your children's favorite toys
- neighborhood animals
- plants from the garden

These can be photos or drawings.

You may select any seven motifs. If, for example, one motif is your dachshund, you may simply take one photograph of him and use seven prints of it. You can also take his photograph in seven different positions.

As a general rule, make sure that photo motifs are easy to recognize and that the backgrounds are clearly distinguishable. Children may have problems when all the photographs use the same green meadow.

If you prefer, the whole family can make drawings.

Be sure that your material is thick enough.

Each motif should have its own background color. For example, when the family paints the mother, the results will probably be very different, and the person may not be recognizable. A uniform background for all seven pictures of the mother makes the game easier later on.

After you glue the motifs on, protect them with clear varnish or with transparent tape.

First Dominoes for Children

You need: 28-tile set and two to four players aged four and up.

The Game

- The players shuffle the face-down tiles and divide them up among themselves.
- The youngest player begins by placing any tile face up in the middle of the table. The other players follow, clockwise.

- The rules of Block Dominoes apply: Anyone who does not have a matching tile has to skip a round.
- The first player to add on all of his tiles wins.

You can also play Domino Lotto with pictures. Use a set with neutral motifs or your family-made dominoes. You'll find the rules on page 18.

Page 62 Magical Squares:

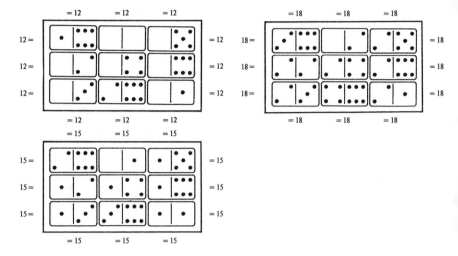

Page 63 Devilish Square:
This is one of the possible solutions.

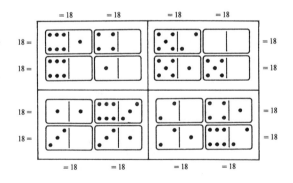

Pages 64 and 65 Blasted 21:

First Task

Second Task

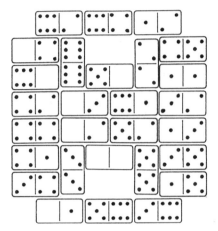

Third Task

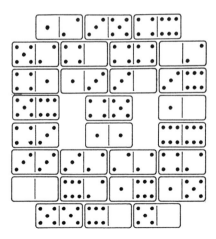

Fourth Task

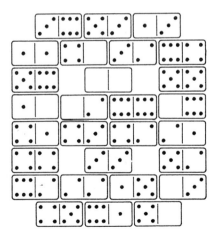

Page 66 Chaos on the Square

First Task

5	1	4	0	2	6	0
1	6	3	0	4	0	4
4	2	2	4	6	2	3
6	5	2	1	5	6	2
1	5	3	6	1	1	0
3	0	3	6	2	1	1
4	2	5	3	5	5	3
4	0	3	6	5	4	0

Second Task

3	5	1	1	3	4	4
3	3	6	4	3	1	4
2	5	1	0	0	1	1
1	3	0	0	0	4	4
1	6	0	0	0	5	2
6	6	6	5	2	6	3
6	6	5	5	2	2	2
4	3	4	5	5	2	2

Page 69 Seven Squares

Page 68 Fraction Dominoes

First Task	Second Task

First Task

$$\frac{3}{4} + \frac{1}{4} + \frac{2}{3} + \frac{1}{3} + \frac{4}{2} = 4$$

$$\frac{2}{5} + \frac{3}{5} + \frac{1}{5} + \frac{4}{5} + \frac{2}{1} = 4$$

$$\frac{2}{6} + \frac{4}{6} + \frac{5}{6} + \frac{1}{6} + \frac{6}{3} = 4$$

Second Task

$$\frac{1}{3} + \frac{6}{1} + \frac{3}{4} + \frac{5}{3} + \frac{5}{4} = 10$$

$$\frac{2}{1} + \frac{5}{1} + \frac{2}{6} + \frac{6}{3} + \frac{4}{6} = 10$$

$$\frac{4}{1} + \frac{2}{3} + \frac{4}{2} + \frac{5}{2} + \frac{5}{6} = 10$$

Page 69 Multiplications

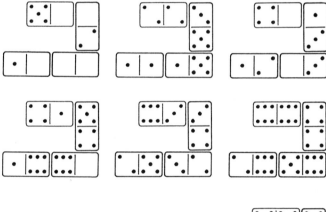

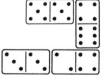

(The task and solution are from Boris A. Kordemsky: *The Moscow Puzzles,* Penguin Books, 1972)

Pages 70–72 Domino Labyrinth:

First Labyrinth   Second Labyrinth

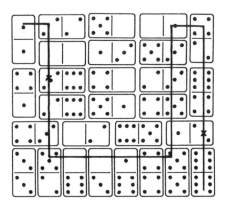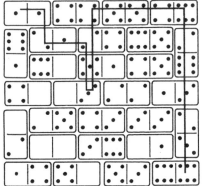

Third Labyrinth   Fourth Labyrinth

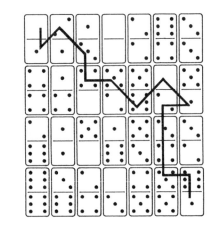

94